GIVE *ideals* THIS CHRISTMAS . . . Let *ideals* express your heartfelt wishes at every season of the year!

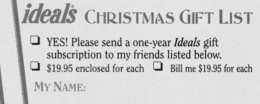

WE'LL ANNOUNCE

D1508452

Every issue of *Ideals* is bursting with a celebration of life's special times: Christmas, Thanksgiving, Easter, Mother's Day, Country and Friendship. Give a gift subscription to *Ideals* this Christmas and you bring joy to the lives of special people six times a year! Each issue offers page after page of magnificent photographs, exquisite drawings and paintings, delightful stories and poetry. Each is a "keeper" that invites the reader back, again and again, to look and read and ponder. There's nothing quite as special as a gift of *Ideals*!

SAVE 44%
off the bookstore price!
To order, mail card at right or call toll-free

1-800-558-4343

ideals CHRISTMAS GIFT LIST

❏ YES! Please send a one-year *Ideals* gift subscription to my friends listed below.
❏ $19.95 enclosed for each ❏ Bill me $19.95 for each
MY NAME:

NAME

ADDRESS

CITY   STATE   ZIP
❏ Please also enter a subscription for myself
SEND A GIFT SUBSCRIPTION TO:

NAME

ADDRESS

CITY   STATE   ZIP
SEND A GIFT SUBSCRIPTION TO:

NAME

ADDRESS

CITY   STATE   ZIP
For addresses outside the U.S.A., annual rate is $25.95 payable in U.S. funds.   C96A

ideals CHRISTMAS GIFT LIST

❏ YES! Please send a one-year *Ideals* gift subscription to my friends listed below.
❏ $19.95 enclosed for each ❏ Bill me $19.95 for each
MY NAME:

NAME

ADDRESS

CITY   STATE   ZIP
❏ Please also enter a subscription for myself
SEND A GIFT SUBSCRIPTION TO:

NAME

ADDRESS

CITY   STATE   ZIP
SEND A GIFT SUBSCRIPTION TO:

NAME

ADDRESS

CITY   STATE   ZIP
For addresses outside the U.S.A., annual rate is $25.95 payable in U.S. funds.   C96B

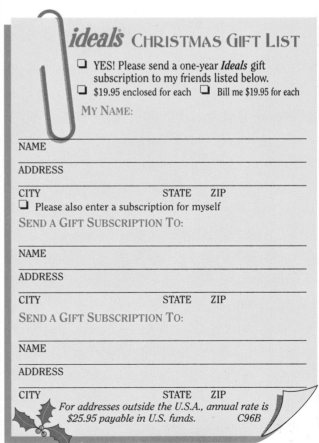

No postage
necessary
if mailed in
the United States

Business Reply Mail
First Class Permit No. 5761 Nashville, TN

POSTAGE WILL BE PAID BY ADDRESSEE

IDEALS PUBLICATIONS INCORPORATED
PO BOX 305300
NASHVILLE TN 37230-9884

No postage
necessary
if mailed in
the United States

Business Reply Mail
First Class Permit No. 5761 Nashville, TN

POSTAGE WILL BE PAID BY ADDRESSEE

IDEALS PUBLICATIONS INCORPORATED
PO BOX 305300
NASHVILLE TN 37230-9884

Do your Christmas shopping today and

SAVE 44%

off the regular bookstore price of *Ideals* when you give a one-year subscription!

Everyone knows at least two or three people who would love a gift subscription to *Ideals*! It's a very special Christmas gift that keeps on reminding a close friend or relative of your thoughtfulness all through the year. And, when you order now, you enjoy a generous savings off the regular bookstore price—and do your Christmas shopping right away!

WE'LL ANNOUNCE YOUR GIFTS WITH GREETING CARDS!

ONLY
$19⁹⁵

for each one-year gift subscription of six issues—a savings of $15.75 off the bookstore price.

To order today, use one or both of the postage-paid reply cards (see reverse side) or call toll-free

1-800-558-4343

Add more gifts, if you wish, by enclosing a separate list with the additional names and addresses and mailing in an envelope to:

Ideals Publications, Inc.
P.O. Box 305300, Nashville, TN 37230

SEND NO MONEY NOW—WE'LL BILL YOU LATER!

Orders received after December 4 will start each subscription with the Easter issue.

ideals® THANKSGIVING

More Than 50 Years of Celebrating Life's Most Treasured Moments

Vol. 53, No. 7

"Cultivate the thankful spirit!
It will be to you a perpetual feast."

—John R. MacDuff

IDEALS—Vol. 53, No. 7 November MCMXCVI IDEALS (ISSN 0019-137X) is published eight times a year:
February, March, May, June, August, September, November, December by
IDEALS PUBLICATIONS INCORPORATED, 535 Metroplex Drive, Suite 250, Nashville, TN 37211.
Periodical postage paid at Nashville, Tennessee, and additional mailing offices.
Copyright © MCMXCVI by IDEALS PUBLICATIONS INCORPORATED.
POSTMASTER: Send address changes to Ideals, PO Box 305300, Nashville, TN 37230. All rights reserved.
Title IDEALS registered U.S. Patent Office.

SINGLE ISSUE—U.S. $5.95 USD; Higher in Canada
ONE-YEAR SUBSCRIPTION—U.S. $19.95 USD; Canada $36.00 CDN (incl. GST and shipping); Foreign $25.95 USD
TWO-YEAR SUBSCRIPTION—U.S. $35.95 USD; Canada $66.50 CDN (incl. GST and shipping); Foreign $47.95 USD

The cover and entire contents of IDEALS are fully protected by copyright and must not be reproduced in any manner whatsoever.

Printed and bound in USA by Quebecor Printing. Printed on Weyerhaeuser Husky.

The paper used in this publication meets the minimum requirements of
American National Standard for Information Sciences—
Permanence of Paper for Printed Library Materials, ANSI Z39.48-1984.

Subscribers may call customer service at 1-800-558-4343 to make address changes.
Unsolicited manuscripts will not be returned without a self-addressed, stamped envelope.

ISBN 0-8249-1140-7   GST 131903775

Cover Photo: HORN OF PLENTY.
Norman Poole Photography.

Inside Front Cover: *LITTLE RED.*
S. Thomas Sierak, artist. Dracut, Massachusetts.

Inside Back Cover: *WEIGHING IN.*
S. Thomas Sierak, artist. Dracut, Massachusetts.

Late Fall

Alice Mackenzie Swaim

Leave the valley to her dreaming,
Wrapped in gold October haze
With her harvest yield around her
As the fires of autumn blaze.

Let the curve of hills enfold her
And the fragrant woodsmoke rise
Like our praise for peace and plenty
To the blue October skies.

PATCHWORK OF AUTUMN
Great Smoky Mountains National Park
North Carolina
Adam Jones Photography

Autumn Trails

Anne Tilley

There is a trail of summer still
That winds around a rugged hill
That the wanderer finds lingering on
Some pale wild asters by a stone.
And in some south-side sheltered place
Are tiny tufts of Queen Anne's lace.
Late milkweed stands with silvered pod
Beside a struggling goldenrod.
In tall, brown grass along the trail
Are vacant nests of vanished quail,
While here and there are leaves of gold
That have escaped November's cold.
Yes, winter's here; still summer clings
To some remote and lovely things.

WOODLAND SERENITY
Porcupine Mountain State Park
Near Ontonagon, Michigan
Josiah Davidson Scenic Photography

Autumn Time

Agnes Davenport Bond

How beautiful are woods and hills,
　Emblazoned now in varied tints
Of bright vermilion, gold, and brown
　Which autumn time imprints.

It also is a fruitful time,
　The harvest of the bloom of spring,
Perfected by the suns and rains
　Which days of summer bring.

Then why should we, when summer wanes,
　With apprehension or dismay
Approach the sunset road that leads
　To life's rich autumn day?

VINE MAPLES IN LAVA ROCK
Willamette National Forest, Oregon
Dennis Frates/Oregon Scenics

Overleaf Photograph
SILVER JACK RESERVOIR
Near Ridgway, Colorado
Josiah Davidson Scenic Photography

The Sapling's Song

Steven R. Jones

Larger trees have sheltered me
   While I have grown in shaded peace.
Their roots have driven deep in storms
   While mine are shallow, soft with ease.

Those greater trees have weathered storms
   And ice and lightning, wind and rain;
So I have grown both tall and straight
   Within the shadows of their pain.

When people come, they look at me
   And praise the well-developed fruit,
But never lift their gaze to see
   The shielded place where I took root.

But time has come and done its work;
   The mighty trees are fading now,
And often lightning strike or gale
   Has splintered trunk or severed bough.

And so at last I start to feel
   The beating sun, the driving hail
And know the dangers in the spring—
   The lightning strikes and blowing gale.

But sturdy, young, and straight am I,
   The product of my elders' care.
It's now my turn to grip the earth
   With stubborn root and do my share.

I have a legacy to keep.
   The ancient forests call my name;
And now I'll stand and hold my ground,
   Remembering those who've done the same.

"Trees of the field will clap their hands,"
   The Master says; and so I shall.
The praise of forests I will give
   To shelter saplings till they're tall.

SHELTERED VINE MAPLE
Mt. Hood National Forest, Oregon
Steve Terrill Photography

BITS & PIECES

When thou hast thanked thy God
 For every blessing sent,
 What time will then remain
 For murmurs or lament?
  —*Archbishop Richard Chenevix Trench*

I thank God for my handicaps; for, through them
 I have found myself, my work, and my God.
  —*Helen Keller*

Heap high the board with plenteous cheer
 And gather to the feast
 And toast the sturdy Pilgrim band
 Whose courage never ceased.
 Give praise to that all-gracious One
 By whom their steps were led,
 And thanks unto the harvest's Lord
 Who sends our daily bread.
  —*Alice Williams Brotherton*

Thank You, dear God,
 For all You have given me,
 For all You have taken away from me,
 For all You have left me.
  —*Author Unknown*

From David learn to give thanks for everything.
Every furrow in the book of Psalms is sown with
the seeds of thanksgiving.
—*Jeremy Taylor*

When you drink from the stream, remember the spring.
—*Chinese Proverb*

And let us give thanks for Someone to thank.
—*Gerhard E. Frost*

We should spend as much time in thanking God for
His benefits as we do in asking Him for them.
—*Vincent De Paul*

Thanksgiving, to be truly thanksgiving,
is first thanks, then giving.
—*Proverb*

Thanksgiving

Margaret Rorke

With harvest in to fill our need,
The year from seed to bloom to seed
Now settles down to sleep.
A sense of having done its best
Provides contentment for its rest—
A sweet reward to reap.

Upon this day of feast and prayer,
Reviewing what we've pleased to share,
May each of us recall
How good is gleaned from planted fields
And love provides surprising yields—
And thank Him for it all.

FALL HARVEST
Gay Bumgarner Photography

OUR HERITAGE

THE MAYFLOWER COMPACT

In the name of God Amen. We whose names are underwritten, the loyall subjects of our dread soveraigne Lord King James by the grace of God, of great Britaine, Franc, and Ireland king, defender of the faith, &c.

Haveing undertaken for the glorie of God, and advancements of the Christian faith and honour of our king & countrie, a voyage to plant the first colonie in the Northerne parts of Virginia, doe by these presents solemnly & mutualy in the presence of God, and one another, covenant & combine our selves togeather into a civill body politick; for our better ordering, & preservation & furtherance of the ends aforesaid; and by vertue hereof to enacte, constitute, and frame shuch just & equall lawes, ordinances, Acts, constitutions, & offices, from time to time, as shall be thought most meete & convenient for the generall good of the Colonie: unto which we promise all due submission and obedience.

In witnes whereof we have hereunder subscribed our names at Cap-Codd the 11 of November, in the year of the raign of our soveraigne Lord King James of England, France, & Ireland, the eighteenth and of Scotland the fiftie fourth. An. Dom. 1620.

ABOUT THE TEXT

In 1620, the *Mayflower* set sail across the Atlantic carrying 102 passengers who intended to settle in territory controlled by the Virginia Company of London. When they found themselves instead landing a good distance north at what is now Cape Cod, Massachusetts, on land beyond the borders controlled by their countrymen, the passengers agreed to sign a covenant guaranteeing government by law, by the consent of the governed. The Mayflower Compact, signed by fifty-one of the ship's male passengers in November of 1620, established self-rule for what would be known as the Plymouth Colony. Only about a third of the *Mayflower*'s passengers were members of the English separatist group called Pilgrims; others came simply seeking new opportunities and new life in America. In time, however, the entire colony became known as Pilgrims, and their courage and perseverance became a cherished and celebrated part of our American heritage.

MBARKATION OF THE PILGRIM
ATHERS AT PLYMOUTH
M. Padory, artist
uperstock

Prayer for Little Things

Jessie Wilmore Murton

Not for the greater burdens
I must bear,
But for the little ones, O Lord,
I make this prayer.

Give patience for the petty
Little cares,
The hasty words and acts that catch
Me unawares.

Give grace to smile, although
My heart be sad,
If it will help to make some other
Dear one glad.

Not for infrequent storms
That cross my way,
But little clouds that dim
The brightness of each day.

Oh, not for greater burdens
I must bear,
But for the little ones, dear Lord,
I make this prayer.

MORNING DELIVERIES
Jacob Taposchaner
FPG International

Readers' Reflections

BLESSINGS

My blessings come from God above;
For God is kind and full of love.
He gives me joy and hope and peace,
From sin and sorrow gives release.

The day is fine, and I am glad.
No grief or sorrow makes me sad.
I hum and sing a happy tune
And to a grandchild softly croon.

My thoughts go far. I humbly pray;
God bless my children every day.

Oh, keep them happy and content
To serve Thee well ere life is spent.

May each one know and love Thee well,
Thy joyous message gladly tell,
That God is love to all mankind.
He sent the Christ, each one to find,

Redeemed us all that we may live
And through our love some blessing give.
For lives are meant to give away
In love and service day by day.

Lillie G. Monter
Loveland, Colorado

NOVEMBER

Briskly tingling, the days have chilled.
With exhilarating crispness the air is filled.
The barren branches of the oaks
Form lacy networks of roughhewn spokes,
Etched in contrast of bolder hue
Against a sky of deepest blue.
Busily engaged are the fallen leaves

In a lively dance with the autumn breeze.
Noisy flocks of feathered races
Gather to travel to warmer places
While those of us they leave behind,
Warmth in hot cider and firesides find.
This the thrill that memory craves
Of refreshingly brisk November days.

Marsha Boston
Waynesburg, Ohio

THANKS FOR THE LITTLE THINGS

I'm thankful for the little things,
The common, take-for-granted things:
    The scent in spring of new-mown hay,
    The sweet perfume from lilac spray,
    The feel of something warm and snug
    Like baby's hand or hubby's hug,
    The taste of Mother's homemade bread,
    Or pumpkin pie will do instead,
    And for this season of the year
    That we can share with friends most dear.
I'm thankful for the little things,

The common, take-for-granted things:
    Two eyes to see all nature's wares
    Displayed from spring to winter bare,
    Two ears to hear the songbird's trill
    Or gentle rain upon the sill,
    Two hands to plant seeds in the dirt
    Or carry balm for someone's hurt,
    Two legs to walk through autumn woods
    And heart to say, "God is so good."
But most of all I'm thankful for
A mind for memories to store.

Lou Ann Mandzuik
Custer, Washington

THE DOVE

I saw it first one frosty morn
On wings of gentle gray
Flying low across the heaven's hue
As dawn broke one autumn day.

A maple tree of crimson red
Bid welcome as it flew.
It landed on a knotty branch
And sang a thankful coo.

Its lyrics, soft but sad to hear,
Lullabied a verse solo.
Across the silvered meadow
Its lonesome song did flow.

The dove seemed to croon farewell
To another season's end;
And on a final, mournful note,
It sailed off in the wind.

Katy Harper
Spencer, West Virginia

AN EARLY WINTER

The golden leaves blend subtly with the brown
And sparkle in the early morning light
As tiny, soft white flakes float gently down
And dawn begins to melt away the night.

Migrating birds, the crispness of the air,
Bright pumpkins, fading hues—all these recall
Excitement of this season oft so fair
And fleeting days that mark the end of fall.

Bare branches now peek out among the trees.
Dry, crackling leaves—more brown than
    e'er before—
Crunch loudly underfoot; and in the breeze,
They whisper of the changes now in store.

The seasons overlap and blend together
As autumn slowly bows to winter's weather.

Shirley Doerfel Whiddon
Simsbury, Connecticut

Thanksgiving Day Prayers

Carol P. Farmer

Receive

our thanks,
O Lord, today.
Bless those here
And those away;
May our hearts
As one be near,
And bless this food
That waits us here.
Keep our thoughts
All pure and clean;
Grant us strength
And grace serene.
In Thy name
We humbly pray;
Bless this good
Thanksgiving Day.

Bless

this food
And table, Lord;
And know that
Thou art most adored.
With grateful hearts
Our thanks we say,
And for Thy grace
We humbly pray.
Keep Thanksgiving
In each heart
To give each day
A rich, new start.
Fill our souls
With peace and cheer,
And bless Thy children
Gathered here.

Bless

us, Lord, who gather here;
Fill this day with thanks and cheer.
Look on each beloved face,
Granting pardon, strength, and grace.
Dwell within our hearts, we pray;
And bless us this Thanksgiving Day.
Keep its joy within each heart
To long remember when we part.
Bless this food we have prepared
As gifts from Thee to now be shared.
We humbly ask for those who came,
All these things, in Jesus' name. Amen.

22

RUSTIC COUNTRY DINING ROOM
Jessie Walker Associates

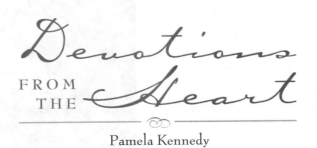

Devotions FROM THE Heart

Pamela Kennedy

In every thing give thanks: for this is the will of God in Christ Jesus concerning you.
–I Thessalonians 5:18

GIVING THANKS

I yanked the rake through the leaves with angry strokes, sending dust and sticks flying. Stopping for a moment, I looked around the yard to assess my progress. When we purchased the house, I had loved the shade offered by the towering oaks and maples. How could I have forgotten that sooner or later those leaves would fall in abundance on our spacious lawn? But it was more than the chore of raking that fed my anger. I had received word that a friend was struggling with a serious illness, and I was angry about the unfairness of suffering. My husband had been called away on a business trip, and I was angry about being left alone. As I meditated on my anger, it grew until I took it out by flailing away at the leaves covering my yard. I needed a break. Maybe a cup of coffee would restore my spirits.

As I relaxed in the kitchen with my coffee, my glance fell on the picture on the refrigerator that my granddaughter had drawn in her Sunday school class. The primitive crayon drawing depicted a scraggly cat sitting on a table. On the floor next to the table was a broken vase, several long-stemmed flowers, and a blue blob I interpreted to be spilled water. Someone had written in neat printing across the bottom of the page: *In every thing give thanks.*

I almost laughed out loud. Give thanks for a yard full of leaves and no one to help me? Give thanks for a friend with a life-threatening illness? And then I looked at the paper again, realizing something that I had missed the first time I read it.

The word was *in,* not *for.*

I sipped my coffee slowly, meditating on the words under the scraggly cat. Could I find a reason for thanks *in* all these circumstances, if not *for* them? I looked out the window at the towering oaks, now filled with bare branches instead of fluttering leaves. A gray squirrel scampered across a limb and into the safety of his snug nest. Thank you Lord, I whispered, for the way you care for all your creatures, great and small. I thought of my dear friend and all the memories we shared; then I whispered a prayer of thanks for her kind and gentle friendship, her sweet example of courage. I smiled recalling the phone conversation I had that morning with my husband and thanked God for such a loving companion. Then my glance rested again on the drawing of the cat, and I was thankful that my children were raising their own children with care and integrity. By the time I had finished the coffee, my anger was gone, dissipated like the steam rising from the teakettle.

With renewed energy, I pulled on my boots and gloves and buttoned my work jacket. Grabbing the rake, I headed for the pile of leaves I had left only a half hour earlier. Somehow the day seemed brighter, the task easier, the wind less threatening. Raising my face to the sky, I thanked God that in the midst of my selfishness, he had spoken His truth and taught me the liberating secret of giving thanks in all things.

Prayer: Dear Father, give me eyes of gratitude that seek, in all circumstances, a reason for giving thanks.

NEIGHBORHOOD IN AUTUMN
Portland, Oregon
Steve Terrill Photography

Thank You, God

Kay Hoffman

Thank you, dear God, for being there
When I sought help from You,
My day so bleak and trouble filled
I knew not what to do.

I breathed Your name in silent prayer,
Made known to You my need.
I sensed You knew my urgency;
I didn't have to plead.

You gave me strength beyond my own
That helped to see me through.
I thank You, God, for being there
Just when I needed You.

WELLS CHURCH
Vermont
Gene Ahrens

Farmer's Prayer

Ardis Rittenhouse

For work that wets my weary brow,
For voices that ask Daddy how,
For burning sun that saps my strength,
For fireplace logs I chop to length,

For fresh-turned earth and fields of green,
For stables that I shovel clean,
For hogs and cows and woolly sheep,
For weariness that lets me sleep,
For the smell of hay, the evening chores,
For creek banks lined with sycamores,
For legs so long they make a lap
Where sleepy heads can take a nap,
For quiet hours, my favorite chair,
For the wife who smiles beside me there,
For churches where the Almighty
Accepts and loves a man like me,
For all these things You've let me touch
I humbly thank You, God, so much!

Shocks of Grain

Craig E. Sathoff

When seasons of the year have come
　　To harvesttime again,
I eagerly look forward to
　　The farmers' shocks of grain.

A shock of grain is made of sheaves
　　Where one leans to the other;

WHEAT HARVEST. Hal Sutherland, artist. Courtesy of the artist and Wild Wings, Inc., Lake City, Minnesota.

And sheaf on sheaf, they lend support
   To strengthen one another.

A shock of grain is molded by
   A farmer's toiling hands,
Is made of love and thankfulness,
   Is product of his land.

And so each shock is meaningful,
   A form of harvest prayer
That stands upright to praise the Lord
   For His abundance there.

HANDMADE HEIRLOOM

BEADED NAPKIN RING. Created by Mary Skarmeas. Jerry Koser Photography.

BEADED NAPKIN RINGS
Mary Skarmeas

Each November, I settle down in my favorite reading chair with a stack of the newest magazines and cookbooks and search their pages for a delicious new recipe to impress my family at Thanksgiving dinner. The glossy photographs flaunt beautiful, dish-laden tables complete with the perfect floral arrangement, hand-lettered place cards, and crisp antique linens. Although my family's Thanksgiving dinners have never been quite this formal and tend toward the "dig in and help yourself" variety, I do think our holiday table could use an added touch of color and charm to complement our favorite holiday fare.

So this year, I put aside my cookbooks and set

out to rediscover the craft of beadwork; the result is a new set of beaded napkin rings in the rich colors of autumn. These simple beaded rings will be just a small part of our annual family feast of Thanksgiving; but they have a unique, rustic appeal, and I plan to make them a permanent fixture on our holiday table.

Beadwork is as old as civilization and has played a part in a variety of beliefs and customs. The first beads were made with an ancient tool called a bow drill, which gave people the ability to pierce ornamental stones. These stone beads were worn around the neck as amulets to ward off evil spirits and disease. Ancient hunters wore beads, made from the teeth and bones of their prey, around their neck in the belief that these beads gave the hunter control over the animal's spirit, imbuing him or her with the courage and strength of the slain prey. Such beads symbolized the hunter's respect for his prey, an acknowledgment of the delicate balance of nature that kept him and his people alive. In many ancient cultures, beads were also significant when one's life ended. Placed alongside the dead, the small trinkets were thought to accompany them into the next life as symbols of their status and achievements on earth. Beyond their ritualistic value, beads often held monetary worth as well: the ancient Egyptians traded with beads made of lapis lazuli, and some groups of Native Americans used wampum—cylindrical beads made from clam shells—as barter.

Artisans in every culture and every age have found a use for the simple and endlessly adaptable bead. Time has transformed the look and feel of the bead—bone, stone, and shell gave way to wood, clay, metal, glass, plastics, and precious stone—but the modern bead, like its ancient predecessor, is any object pierced through it center for stringing. Today, beads come in almost every size, material, and color. They handsomely adorn our necks, decorate our homes, and inspire our imagination. For some craftspeople, the bead itself is a work of art, each one produced by hand to be unlike any other. To others, colorful, mass-produced beads are the raw materials awaiting their inspiration.

These mass-produced beads have sparked a revival of traditional bead crafts. Craft stores are stocking their shelves with the most amazing variety of beads, from tiny, single-colored plastic ones to chunky wooden ones to delicate ones of hand-painted ceramic. Today's beaders are making jewelry, bookmarks, and picture frames; they are using beads together with embroidery to decorate their clothing; and they are creating one-of-a-kind Christmas ornaments and other holiday decorations—all sporting the glorious colors and patterns that beadwork offers.

My Thanksgiving napkin rings were inspired by the season, by a book on beading, and by several visits to local craft stores to browse through the rainbow of colorful beads. I used the general instructions from one of many books on beading to get me started, but the final design turned out to be my own as I personalized what I saw on the page. A book or an experienced beader will get the newcomer started on the right foot; visit a small craft store that stocks a good supply of beads and ask for help. Most of all, be patient! Like any new craft, beadwork feels awkward at first; but as your hands begin to get the feel of it, beading is a lovely leisure time hobby for anyone who likes close work and lovely detail.

Beadwork has a unique appeal to craftspeople of all ages, interests, and skill levels. Not only is beading done by the most highly skilled artisans, but it is also often a favorite project of young children at summer camp. Anyone can be inspired by the wonderful sight of store shelves packed with blocks of colorful beads!

My family's Thanksgiving table has always been filled with warm, nourishing food made by loving hands. Now the plentiful dishes will be joined by my beautiful beaded napkin rings, which will last long after the last turkey sandwich disappears with a hungry grandchild. I am certain that my colorful beaded rings will add a charming, homemade touch to our holiday table and become a unique part of all our happy Thanksgiving traditions.

Mary Skarmeas lives in Danvers, Massachusetts, and has recently earned her bachelor's degree in English at Suffolk University. Mother of four and grandmother of two, Mary loves all crafts, especially knitting.

Home for Thanksgiving

Angela Gall

A hundred miles of singing road
Where hill-caped farmlands fall and rise
With gaping bins of yellow grain
And pumpkin gold and harvest skies,
The hillside home the heart knows well,
The warmth where open arms await,
The sweets and spice all nostril-nice,
The turkey-stuffing-laden plate—
This feast with loved ones a world away,
All mine by journey of heart today.

VILLAGE THANKSGIVING
East Orange, Vermont
Josiah Davidson Scenic Photography

Ideals' Family Recipes

Favorite Recipes from the Ideals Family of Readers

Editor's Note: Please send us your best-loved recipes! Mail a typed copy of the recipe along with your name, address, and phone number to Ideals magazine, ATTN: Recipes, P.O. Box 305300, Nashville, Tennessee 37230. We will pay $10 for each recipe used. Recipes cannot be returned.

PUMPKIN NUT BARS

Preheat oven to 350° F. In a large bowl, sift together 1 cup all-purpose flour, ½ teaspoon baking powder, ½ teaspoon baking soda, and 1½ teaspoons pumpkin pie spice; set aside. In a separate bowl, cream 1 cup firmly packed brown sugar with ½ cup shortening. Add ⅔ cup cooked, mashed pumpkin and 2 beaten eggs. Add flour mixture. With an electric mixer on medium speed, beat 1 minute or until mixture is smooth. Stir in 1 cup chopped pecans. Pour batter into a greased and floured, 9-by-13-by-2-inch baking pan; bake 25 to 30 minutes or until a wooden pick inserted into center comes out clean. Cool; sprinkle with powdered sugar. Cut into bars. Makes 2½ dozen bars.

Rebekah I. Miller
Rocky Mount, Virginia

PUMPKIN COOKIES

Preheat oven to 375° F. In a large bowl, sift together 2 cups all-purpose flour, 1 teaspoon baking powder, ½ teaspoon baking soda, 1 teaspoon ground cinnamon, ½ teaspoon allspice, and ½ teaspoon salt. Set aside. In a large bowl, cream 1 cup butter or shortening with 1 cup granulated sugar. Add 1 cup cooked, mashed pumpkin; 1 egg; and 1 teaspoon vanilla. Stir well. Add flour mixture; mix well. Fold in 1 cup chopped nuts and 1 cup raisins. Drop batter by spoonfuls onto a well-greased baking sheet; bake 15 minutes. Cool on wire racks. Makes 5 dozen cookies.

Susan Aresco
Middletown, Connecticut

PUMPKIN BREAD

Preheat oven to 350° F. In a large bowl, sift together 3½ cups all-purpose flour, 3 cups granulated sugar, 1½ teaspoons salt, 2 teaspoons baking soda, 1 teaspoon ground cinnamon, and 1 teaspoon ground nutmeg. Add 1 cup applesauce; 4 eggs; 2 cups cooked, mashed pumpkin; ⅔ cup water; and 1 cup nuts, beating well after each addition. Pour batter into two 8-by-4-by-2-inch loaf pans, and bake 1 hour. Makes two loaves.

Janice Leilani Smith
Kingsville, Texas

PUMPKIN CHIP MUFFINS

Preheat oven to 400° F. In a large bowl, combine 4 eggs, 2 cups granulated sugar, one 16-ounce can pumpkin, and 1½ cups vegetable oil. Beat until smooth; set aside. In a large bowl, sift together 3 cups all-purpose flour, 2 teaspoons baking soda, 2 teaspoons baking powder, 1 teaspoon ground cinnamon, and 1 teaspoon salt. Slowly add flour mixture to pumpkin mixture, stirring well. Fold in one 12-ounce bag butterscotch or semisweet chocolate chips. Fill greased or paper-lined muffin cups with batter until three-fourths full. Bake 16 to 20 minutes or until centers of muffins bounce back when touched. Cool in pan 10 minutes; remove to wire rack. Makes approximately 24 muffins.

Sophia Boyer
York, Pennsylvania

PUMPKIN DESSERT

Preheat oven to 350° F. In a large bowl, combine 1 cup sifted, all-purpose flour; ½ cup quick-cooking oats; and ½ cup brown sugar. With a pastry blender, cut in ½ cup butter or margarine until mixture resembles coarse crumbs. Press onto bottom of an ungreased, 9-by-13-by-2-inch baking pan. Bake 15 minutes.

In a large bowl, combine 2 cups cooked, mashed pumpkin; one 12-ounce can evaporated milk; 2 eggs; ¾ cup granulated sugar; 1 tablespoon melted butter or margarine; 1 teaspoon cinnamon; ¼ teaspoon ground cloves; ¼ teaspoon ground nutmeg; and ½ teaspoon salt. Stir well. Pour mixture over crust and return to oven 20 minutes.

In a small bowl, cream 2 tablespoons butter or margarine with ½ cup firmly packed brown sugar. Stir in ½ cup chopped walnuts. Sprinkle mixture over top of dessert; return to oven 15 minutes. Cool. Serve with whipped cream. Makes about 12 servings.

Lydia J. Miller
Garnett, Kansas

THEME IN YELLOW

Carl Sandburg

I spot the hills
With yellow balls in autumn.
I light the prairie cornfields
Orange and tawny gold clusters
And I am called pumpkins.
On the last of October
When dusk is fallen
Children join hands
And circle round me
Singing ghost songs
And love to the harvest moon;
I am a jack-o'-lantern
With terrible teeth
And the children know
I am fooling.

The unique perspective of Russ Flint's artistic style has made him a favorite of Ideals readers for many years. A resident of California and father of four, Russ Flint has illustrated a children's Bible and many other books.

THE PUMPKIN

John Greenleaf Whittier

Ah! on Thanksgiving Day,
　　When from East and from West,
From North and from South
　　Come the Pilgrim and guest,
When the gray-haired New Englander
　　Sees round his board
The old broken links
　　Of affection restored,
When the care-wearied man
　　Seeks his mother once more,
And the worn matron smiles
　　Where the girl smiled before,
What moistens the lip
　　And what brightens the eye?
What calls back the past
　　Like the rich pumpkin pie?
Oh—fruit loved of boyhood—
　　The old days recalling,
When wood-grapes were purpling
　　And brown nuts were falling!
When wild, ugly faces
　　We carved in its skin,
Glaring out through the dark
　　With a candle within!
When we laughed round the corn-heap,
　　With hearts all in tune,
Our chair a broad pumpkin,
　　Our lantern the moon,
Telling tales of a fairy
　　Who traveled like steam,
In a pumpkin-shell coach,
　　With two rats for her team!

BOUNTIFUL HARVEST
Jane Wooster Scott, artist
Superstock

JELLY-MAKING TIME

Alice Mackenzie Swaim

It's jelly-making time!
The copper pans are polished, ready for the gleaming fruit.
The kitchen smells sweet as a summer meadow
As Mother stirs the fruit and skims the foam
Into an old, cracked saucer.

We get in her way,
Asking for tastes and carefully not touching
The glasses lined up on the kitchen table.
The rich juice dripped all night from cheesecloth bags;
We dare not squeeze to mar its pure translucency.

By suppertime,
Glasses and jars are labeled, put away,
All but one dish to eat with homemade bread.
The jeweled colors gleam on cellar shelves,
A summer rainbow for bleached winter days.

A SLICE OF LIFE

Edgar A. Guest

RAISIN PIE

There's a heap of pent-up goodness
    In the yellow bantam corn,
And I sort o' like to linger
    Round a berry patch at morn;
Oh, the Lord has set our table
    With a stock o' things to eat,
An' there's just enough o' bitter
    In the blend to cut the sweet;
But I run the whole list over,
    An' it seems somehow that I
Find the keenest sort o' pleasure
    In a chunk o' raisin pie.

There are pies that start the water
    Circulatin' in the mouth;
There are pies that wear the flavor
    Of the warm an' sunny south;
Some with oriental spices
    Spur the drowsy appetite
An' just fill a fellow's being
    With a thrill o' real delight;
But for downright, solid goodness
    That comes drippin' from the sky,
There is nothing quite the equal
    Of a chunk o' raisin pie.

'm admittin' tastes are diff'rent,
    I'm not settin' up myself
As the judge an' final critic
    Of the good things on the shelf.
'm just sort of payin' tribute
    To a simple joy on earth,
ort o' feebly testifyin'
    To its lasting charm an' worth,
An' I'll hold to this conclusion
    Till it comes my time to die,
hat there's no dessert that's finer
    Than a chunk o' raisin pie.

Edgar A. Guest began his illustrious career in 1895 at the age of fourteen when his work first appeared in the Detroit Free Press. His column was syndicated in over three hundred newspapers, and he became known as "The Poet of the People."

Patrick McRae is an artist who lives in the Milwaukee, Wisconsin, area. He has created nostalgic artwork for Ideals for more than a decade, and his favorite models are his wife and three children.

Thanksgiving Dinner

Gladys Taber

When the children come home for Thanksgiving, out comes the big roaster. Dinner is traditional, including fluffy turnips, cranberry sauce, giblet gravy, mashed potatoes. We do not, however, have the mince and apple pies. This is a sign of the times, for the children count the calories and prefer to use them up on the main dinner. The small ones have dishes of ice cream while the adults have a fruit bowl, cheese, and crackers.

Toward evening, everyone is ready for cold turkey and thinly sliced dressing for sandwiches. It is self-service, for Mama is through for the day! Later we get out the corn popper and a bowl of apples, in case anyone is starving. We like corn popped in a rusty popper from the early days, shaken back and forth over the embers in the fireplace. I use part oil and part butter and more salt than anyone would believe. My feeling is the oil spreads the butter more evenly—but this may be another of my notions.

It is a happy holiday and a reminder that we owe thanks to the forefathers who struggled in the alien land to find a foothold and establish a community.

I remember when turkey was a once-in-a-year dinner. It symbolized Thanksgiving. Ham was for Easter, along with eggs cooked in fancy ways. Roast beef and Yorkshire pudding meant Christmas in our house when I was growing up, or stuffed goose when Mama could get it.

Our turkey came from a farm near Black Creek, I believe; and I stood around waiting to see Father bring it in the house. Then that delicious smell of sage and onion and savory filled the house as Mama stuffed his majesty and tucked him in the gas oven (allowing plenty of time for the gas to die down around suppertime as it always did).

Nowadays turkey is so available it is no longer a seasonal treat. At times I am sorry it is so common, for that first thrill of seeing it on Thanksgiving morning is gone. The grandchildren accept turkey as just another good meal. I won't go so far as to say it should be restricted to holidays; but a few things should still be rare treats, I think. Of course it always is a treat to me because, since I live alone, the only turkey I meet is when the children assemble for a weekend or a holiday. One person, even with the help of an Irish and cockers, cannot undertake even a small turkey. The half turkeys now available are fine apartment dwellers but still too much for me.

THROUGH MY WINDOW

Pamela Kennedy

Art by Russ Flint

TRUE THANKFULNESS

E very year, when November rolls around and Thanksgiving plans begin, I recall the Thanksgiving my husband and I first learned about real thankfulness.

It was a crisp fall in Newport, Rhode Island, twenty-one years ago. We lived in a two-story duplex in a Navy housing area and were new parents with a six-month-old son. Our neighbors were all just about like us: young couples starting out in the Navy, away from home, filled with hopes and dreams of family, patriotism, and a bright future. The men spent their days in classes together and their evenings huddled over diagrams of engineering

plants, training to become department heads on ships. We women grew close sharing joys and concerns about the Navy, our own careers, and our children. When November arrived, several of us decided to join together at one home for a big, old-fashioned Thanksgiving dinner. Randy, a Navy lieutenant, and his wife Karla offered to host the event, and plans were made. Each couple was to supply a family favorite for the Thanksgiving table, and everyone donated a few dollars so Karla could buy a gigantic turkey we dubbed "Moby Dick." Despite the fact that none of us would be going home for Thanksgiving, we were excited about planning and executing our Navy family feast.

The day before Thanksgiving, Randy skipped his morning classes to go to sick call. He had a lingering headache, and his vision in one eye was unclear. Karla chalked it up to over-zealous study habits. The doctor thought otherwise, however, and ordered a set of x-rays. By two o'clock that afternoon, Randy was on a plane headed for the Naval hospital in Bethesda, Maryland, with a mysterious brain tumor.

The news spread through our close-knit community like a malevolent cloud. We were young, successful high-achievers with our futures spread before us like a bright path. No one had dreamed the path might take a dangerous turn or drop off into an abyss of death. Now we looked at one another differently, forced to acknowledge this darker possibility.

With the optimism of youth, we assured one another it would probably prove to be nothing serious—a benign lesion, easily removed. After all, Randy had plans, places to go, people to see. His one-year-old daughter, Joy, needed her daddy to bounce her on his knee and show her the sunset from the bridge of the ship he would one day command.

By Tuesday night, we had the preliminary diagnosis: a rare form of cancer had invaded Randy's brain. On Wednesday, the sun came up as usual. Men went to classes. Women went to work or cared for their children. Meanwhile the malignancy that worked its dark way into Randy's brain slithered into our minds as well. If this could happen to one of us, it could happen to any of us. Husbands and wives hugged each other a little longer at the doorway, kissed their children more tenderly, spoke in softer tones. We were forced to confront the fragility of our future, the ethereal quality of our security.

Karla left Joy with a neighbor and dropped off "Moby Dick" at my house on her way to the airport to join Randy.

"Please go ahead and have Thanksgiving at our house," she implored through her tears. "It would mean a lot to Randy and me. Besides, Moby Dick is half thawed."

I hugged Karla, promised we would all pray for them, waved good-bye as she drove off, and wept over the huge, glistening turkey that was dripping on my kitchen counter. How could we be thankful together in their home when they were facing life and death in a sterile hospital room alone?

On Thanksgiving Day, ten young families gathered around a table laden with dozens of savory delicacies. In the corner, on his own table, surrounded with bowls of stuffing and gravy, Moby Dick waited to be carved. We joined hands, bowed our heads, and prayed together, thanking God for His bounty, His goodness to us all, His unchangeable ways. Then one young officer asked God's mercy on our dear friends Randy, Karla, and little Joy.

We feasted together that afternoon on turkey and all the trimmings; but for many of us, it was the first time we had truly savored the sweetness of life. We relished each conversation, treasured each friend a bit more, reflected upon our blessings with greater thoughtfulness.

As we divided up the leftovers, the phone rang. It was Randy. "Just want you guys to know the doc thinks he got it all and was able to leave enough of my brain for me to still be a threat for the class competition! Don't give away my study desk yet!" Amid laughter and tears, the phone was passed around; and when the call ended, we stood looking at each other in an awkward silence. Then someone said "Thank You, God, for Your faithfulness to us."

It was a humble, heartfelt prayer echoing our mutual wonder and gratitude for God's goodness. The intervening years would take us to distant places far from the security of family and friends. Our lives would be defined by the caprices of war and politics. Our security would never be found in place or time. Yet in the midst of life's uncertainties, we had discovered the anchor that could hold us fast: the unending faithfulness of our God. It was good to give thanks.

Pamela Kennedy is a freelance writer of short stories, articles, essays, and children's books. Wife of a Naval officer and mother of three children, she has made her home on both U.S. coasts and currently resides in Honolulu, Hawaii. She draws her material from her own experiences and memories, adding highlights from her imagination to enhance the story.

In a Field of Bittersweet

Violet Alleyn Storey

Here I have come, oh, very close to God
In this high field festooned with bittersweet.
Both summer and fall are done, and autumn now
Creeps up this hill on silent, frost-shod feet.

And I give thanks that in my heart today,
Time-harvested, the hours of peace and strife
Are linked as here are linked the earth and sky
By the enduring bittersweet of life.

CLIMBING BITTERSWEET AND
VIRGINIA CREEPER
Quabbin Reservoir, Massachusetts
William Johnson/Johnson's Photography

My November Guest

Robert Frost

My Sorrow, when she's here with me,
    Thinks these dark days of autumn rain
Are beautiful as days can be;
She loves the bare, the withered tree;
    She walks the sodden pasture lane.

Her pleasure will not let me stay.
    She talks and I am fain to list:
She's glad the birds are gone away,
She's glad her simple worsted gray
    Is silver now with clinging mist.

The desolate, deserted trees,
    The faded earth, the heavy sky,
The beauties she so truly sees,
She thinks I have no eye for these,
    And vexes me for reason why.

Not yesterday I learned to know
    The love of bare November days
Before the coming of the snow,
But it were vain to tell her so,
    And they are better for her praise.

SCADES AMID AUTUMN COLOR
ltnomah Falls, Oregon
nnis Frates/Oregon Scenics

My Favorite Thanksgiving Memory

Personal Stories of Treasured Memories from the Ideals Family of Readers

Thanksgiving at the Lake

As a child, I eagerly awaited visits to my Uncle Elbert and Aunt Bertie who lived on a farm in western Tennessee. When I was twelve years old, my uncle wrote my mother to ask if I could spend Thanksgiving with him and my aunt, and my mother agreed. As the day approached for my bus ride, my excitement grew. The year was 1930, a time when luxuries were scarce; and the invitation to visit the farm came as an unexpected pleasure.

The bus trip took nearly an hour; but it seemed much longer to me as I watched the Autumn trees speed by and felt my anticipation escalate as the bus approached the station. My uncle was waiting to greet me, and we soon began our drive to his country home.

A boy at heart, Uncle Elbert liked to tease; and often I did not know when he was serious and when he was just waiting for my gullible response. This was the case as we rode toward his home that day and he suddenly said, "We're going to Reelfoot Lake for Thanksgiving!" I was shocked to realize he was not joking.

Uncle Elbert was an avid fisherman and thought that Reelfoot Lake was the greatest place in the world. I had been there several times during my summer visits and enjoyed it—but Thanksgiving at Reelfoot? I had pictured this holiday much differently, and I tried to conceal my disappointment. During my long bus trip, I had eagerly visualized Aunt Bertie's table—set with her best linens, china, and silver—and a scrumptious dinner of chicken and dressing, home-baked rolls, sweet potatoes with marshmallows, homemade relishes, savory vegetables, and several cakes and pies. Before she married my uncle, Aunt Bertie had been a home economics teacher; and I thought she was the best cook in the world. In fact, I still use many of her tried and true recipes.

When we arrived at the large white frame house, Aunt Bertie ran out to greet me; and I was thrilled to discover that my great-grandmother, Mother Hill, was visiting also. Tall, thin, and stately looking, she had the sweetest smile I had ever seen.

On Thanksgiving morning, I awoke to a beautiful, unusually pleasant day for November; and in spite of my trepidation, I began to feel a sense of adventure as we packed the car and headed toward the lake.

As soon as we arrived, Uncle Elbert was off in a boat and ready to fish. Aunt Bertie and Mother Hill began to unpack the iron skillet, lard, and cornmeal for frying his prize catch; and

I prepared a nearby picnic table with a red and white checkered cloth, old dishes, and old forks and knives.

In a surprisingly short time, Uncle Elbert returned proudly with a good catch of fish. Aunt Bertie had already started a fire, and she placed sweet potatoes among the coals to roast while Mother Hill and I unpacked coleslaw, corn lightbread, fruitcake, and pumpkin pie from the basket. Over the fire, a pot of coffee sat on a rack and filled the cool air with a tantalizing smell.

As the fish sizzled, I looked up at the tall pines and soon forgot my previous vision of what I had expected the day to be. The food was made only more delicious by the beauty of nature and our peaceful surroundings.

In my mind's eye, I can still vividly see all of us smiling and laughing as we shared our unique Thanksgiving meal and looked out over the quiet lake with its knotty cypress knees protruding from the water. The image of that special day will remain in my memory forever.

Lila B. Mullins
Nashville, Tennessee

A Time To Remember

I have vivid memories of one Thanksgiving when I was young. To celebrate the occasion, my mother's entire family gathered together at the home of Uncle George and Aunt Bertha, who lived on a small farm outside the village of Morris, Michigan, about twenty miles from our home town. Since there were very few automobiles in those days, our family made the trip on the Grand Trunk Railroad. What a sight it must have been to see Mother, Dad, and seven kids, along with several baskets of food, scramble to find seats in the train coach! When we reached our destination, Uncle George was waiting to load us onto a horse and wagon for our drive to his farm.

All the relatives began arriving, and the house was soon overflowing with people. My mother had seven children; Aunt Bertha had nine; Aunt Pearl had four; Mother's half sister, Aunt Blanche, had ten; and her other half sister, Aunt Delma, had two. There were cousins by the dozens!

Soon the women and young adults were busy in the kitchen preparing food and arranging the tables and chairs. The men were visiting in the parlor or out in the farmyard; and we kids had the entire second floor to ourselves, where we were free to play, shout, and laugh to our hearts' content.

Finally the magical moment arrived, and we were called to the dining room for the Thanksgiving feast. What a bountiful table—chicken and duck, dressing, potatoes, gravy, home-canned vegetables, homemade pickles, jellies, jams, fresh-baked bread and rolls. I remember being awed by the mouth-watering display of desserts: pumpkin and mincemeat pies, cakes, cookies, and gelatin with whipped cream. Oh, how we all enjoyed the food!

All too quickly, it was time to leave; and our family, happy and tired, trooped onto the train for the homeward journey. As children, we might not have understood the real meaning of the holiday; but we were definitely thankful for a day filled with warm, delicious food and glorious childhood fun.

Cecile Bernath
Chelsea, Michigan

Editor's Note: Do you have a special holiday or seasonal memory that you'd like to share with the *Ideals* family of readers? We'd love to read it! Send your typed memory to:

My Favorite Memory
c/o Editorial Department
Ideals Magazine
535 Metroplex Drive, Suite 250
Nashville, Tennessee 37211

All Through November

Ruth Van Gorder

EARLY AUTUMN SNOW ON 4TH STREET. Steven R. Kozar, artist. Courtesy of the artist and Wild Wings, Inc., Lake City, Minnesota.

All through November, heaven by day
Wraps itself closely in ominous gray.
All through November, evening wind whines
Wistfully, woefully over the pines.
All through November, rain cold as sleet
Puts out the leaf fires warming its feet.
All through November, weather has woes
And will not be happy until it snows.

Mildred Smithson

AN AFTERNOON IN AUTUMN
Acadia National Park, Maine

Autumn on the Maine coast is magnificent. We spent the week at Acadia National Park, most of which is on Mount Desert Island. The island's name is deceptive. French explorer Samuel de Champlain named it *L'Isle des Monts Deserts* in honor of the smooth granite domes that top its peaks, but Mount Desert Island is anything but a barren desert. Thick forests run right up to the water's edge, where rocky cliffs and inlets break the waves of the Atlantic Ocean. It is a sight rarely duplicated on the American coastline; no sand dunes, no marshes—just forest, rock, and sea.

The view from Cadillac Mountain—the highest point on the eastern American coastline—is absolutely breathtaking. We were surprised to learn that the autumn display of reds, oranges, yellows, and golds mixing with the deep greens of the spruces, pines, and balsam firs is a recent development on Mount Desert Island. The Great Fire of 1947 burned more than 17,000 acres of prime evergreen forest on the island but provided opportunity for sun-loving maples, aspens, and birches to flourish on the fertile, fire-charred slopes. Champlain might have named the island differently if he could have seen it on a crisp, clear autumn day like today!

CADILLAC MOUNTAIN
Mount Desert Island
Acadia National Park, Maine
Adam Jones Photography

Borrowed Beauty

Anna M. Priestley

November borrowed this bright day from April,
This sun and shower and lightly winging breeze,
This bow of promise, ending in the meadows,
These torn, gray veils, caught on the distant trees.

The tattered remnants of October's splendor
Still cling to sumac and to vines profuse,
To a few valiant wayside oaks and maples
And grapes, still husbanding their purple juice.

Only the ordered rows of corn shocks, standing,
Heaps of their own gold lying at their feet,
Belong to the bare landscape of November,
These and the emerald fields of winter wheat.

This is a day to treasure in the mem'ry
When bushes crouch in fleecy coats of snow,
A day to furnish fuel in December
To kindle in the heart a warming glow.

VINEYARD'S BOUNTY
Alpine Vineyards, Oregon
Dennis Frates/Oregon Scenics

Late Autumn

Isla Paschal Richardson

Autumn has come again. The time each year
When yellow leaves are falling. Johnson grass
Has gone to seed, but let no farmer hear
Me praise its graceful scepters where it crowds
The edges of the fences. And the skies
Are very, very blue while soft white clouds
Pile high and billowy. Large butterflies
Flit hurriedly, uncertain where to go.
The royal colors of the ironweed
And goldenrod are fading. All aglow
Are sunsets. On the dogwood trees the seed
Are bright red clusters. It has come again—
The season that is whispering "Amen."

JAPANESE MAPLE
Charlie Borland/F-Stock, Inc.

LEGENDARY AMERICANS

PATRICIA A. PINGRY

GEORGE GERSHWIN

Serious American music didn't exist before George Gershwin. When he was born, popular music was the lush and sentimental melodies of Victor Herbert, Caruso was the most popular tenor, opera was Italian, and jazz was played only by black musicians in out-of-the-way places. George Gershwin changed music, American music, forever; and his songs continue to touch our lives.

"You say eether and I say eyether, /You say neether /And I say nyther." Born Jacob Gershwine on September 26, 1898, at the family home in Brooklyn, the younger son of Morris and Rose arrived about five years after his father left czarist Russia for New York's Lower East Side. The family wasn't poor; but Morris and Rose pinned their hopes for financial advancement on Ira, the older and bookish son. Young George was early considered a failure who would amount to little.

"They all laughed at Christopher Columbus/ When he said the world was round . . . /But ho, ho, ho, who's got the last laugh now." The young Gershwin liked to play hooky, fight, and wrestle; he hated to read and felt no need to study. One day, the twelve-year-old had just sneaked out of school to avoid a violin recital when he heard the opening notes of the violin. Young George was instantly captivated by the sound and from that moment on devoted his life to music. Years later, George recalled the moment: "It was to me, a flashing revelation of beauty."

"Liza, Liza, skies are gray. /But if you'll smile on me /All the clouds'll roll away." In 1910, the Gershwins bought a piano for Ira, but it was George who startled his family by sitting down and playing a popular tune. Rose provided for piano lessons, thinking it would instill discipline in her wayward boy; his father had seen his son's future as a scoundrel and thought even playing the piano was a preferable alternative. George developed quickly as an accomplished pianist, given to flair and able to play even the most difficult passages. At fifteen, he left school, where his only success had been in playing for the morning assembly, and took a job at a music publishing house.

"I got rhythm, /I got music, /I got my man /Who could ask for anything more?" Gershwin's days were now spent playing other composers' tunes for show people to consider using in their acts. George, probably out of boredom, added chords and arpeggios, changed keys; yet he was constantly reminded that he was only the piano player, not the composer he longed to be.

"Swanee, /How I love you, /How I love you, /My dear old Swanee." At twenty-one, Gershwin was still looking for the *big* song to make him famous. Nobody paid much attention to one, written with lyricist Irving Caesar, about a mythical southern river named Swanee, until Al Jolson sang it on Broadway. An instant hit, the record sold one million copies. Never again would Gershwin have such a huge commercial success.

"I'll build a stairway to Paradise /With a new step every day!" Early in his career, Gershwin collaborated with several lyricists, but his lasting partnership was with brother Ira. The two brothers began a routine with George at the piano and Ira at the table, both sweating over words and music. Their first song together was "The Real American Folk Song" which was a precursor of things to come.

"Someday he'll come along /The man I love; /And he'll be big and strong, /The man I love." In November

64

1923, mezzo-soprano Eve Gauthier gave a program of ancient and modern music, and among the modern composers was George Gershwin. By the time Miss Gauthier got to Gershwin's portion of the recital, many in the audience were showing signs of boredom. Gershwin replaced her standard accompanist for the American compositions, and the audience sensed a new direction for the concert.

"Oh, sweet and lovely lady, be good! /O lady, be good to me!" The program's modern section began with several popular but tired compositions then moved on to Gershwin's "I'll Build a Stairway to Paradise" and concluded with "Swanee." At that point, the audience went wild, and the two returned for encores. Overnight, Gershwin, at only twenty-five, was judged a serious composer by the critics, by the press, by the world.

"'Swonderful! 'Smarvelous! /You should care for me! /'Sawful nice, 'Sparadise! /'Swhat I love to see!" The following year, Gershwin sealed his preeminence in American music. Paul Whiteman gave "An Experiment in Modern Music" and publicized "a new jazz concerto" by Gershwin. This whole episode was unplanned, and few other composers could or would have composed a piece in the short time allowed. Gershwin, always optimistic and eager to please fans and friends, took about three weeks.

"Embrace me, My sweet embraceable you! /Embrace me, You irreplaceable you!" Whiteman's concert got off to a lively start but, like Gauthier's before it, soon bogged down in mediocre compositions; and the bored audience began heading toward the exits. Then Gershwin stepped up to the piano for his portion. He nodded to Whiteman, who pointed to the clarinetist, whose glissando began the "jazz concerto." The effect was electrifying. The composition was *Rhapsody in Blue*.

"Somebody loves me I wonder who, /I wonder who she can be." Gershwin's next big triumph was *An American in Paris*. He had met the great French composer Maurice Ravel in New York. Gershwin took Ravel to hear jazz in Harlem, and Ravel provided Gershwin with a letter of introduction to a renowned French music teacher. Ironically, Gershwin, who found school boring, never stopped studying music.

"Summertime—an' the livin' is easy, /Fish are jumpin' an' the cotton is high." Gershwin had now conquered Broadway with several hit shows, written songs the whole country was humming, but still longed to write an opera. In 1932 he reached an agreement with the author of the novel *Porgy*, DuBose Heyward, to collaborate on the opera. When Gershwin visited a black church in Heyward's hometown in South Carolina, he was excited by what he heard. A dozen voices, each starting at a different time, were raised in loud rhythmic prayer, forming a clearly defined pattern. The words were lost, but the effect was a pounding rhythm, terrifying in its intensity. Gershwin would re-create this effect in *Porgy*'s storm scene.

"Oh I got plenty o' nuttin', /An' nuttin's plenty fo' me. /I got no car, got no mule, /I got no misery." Gershwin insisted *Porgy* be performed almost completely with black performers, meaning the usual opera outlets were bypassed. *Porgy* floundered at the box office, and music critics generally panned the music, saying Gershwin had created a night of songs, not an opera. The venture was a financial disaster.

"They're writing songs of love, /But not for me. /A lucky star's above, /But not for me." After *Porgy*, both Gershwins went to Hollywood to write for the movies. George soon complained of headaches, extreme fatigue, and evidenced erratic behavior; and doctors attributed his condition to his emotional state. At one point, as Gershwin left a restaurant with friends, he fell and couldn't get up. One of his companions stepped over the composer and, amazingly, remarked, "Leave him there, all he wants is attention." Finally, a doctor recognized the symptoms, and emergency surgery revealed the truth. At the age of thirty-eight and at the height of his creativity, George Gershwin had a malignant brain tumor. After the operation, he lapsed into a coma and died two days later.

"The way you wear your hat, /The way you sip your tea, /The mem'ry of all that, /No, No! They can't take that away from me!" At the time, novelist John O'Hara said, "George Gershwin died on July 11, 1937, but I don't have to believe it if I don't want to." The world has not allowed Gershwin's music to die. In 1976 the Houston Grand Opera presented a stunning production of *Porgy and Bess* with the original score and orchestration intact. The production was a triumph which brought the shock of recognition: *Porgy and Bess* was a real opera. In 1985 the New York's Metropolitan Opera House gave the ultimate endorsement by their performance. Today's critics universally acknowledge *Porgy and Bess* as an operatic triumph, *An American in Paris* a Broadway masterpiece, and *Rhapsody in Blue* the wake-up call for American composers.

"It's very clear /Our love is here to stay; /Not for a year, /But ever and a day." The world has rediscovered Gershwin's art and fallen in love again with his music. They love its excitement, its sophistication, its warmth. And when *Rhapsody in Blue* begins its clarinet glissando, the shivers that race down the spine of every listener are a physical reminder that George Gershwin lives.

Nature's Music

Carice Williams

The sweetest music oft is heard
By nature's symphony.
The sound of waves upon the shore,
A songbird in a tree,
The whisp'ring wind, the falling rain,
And crickets in the fall
Add to the harmony that plays
The sweetest song of all.

"There's music
  In the sighing of a reed;
There's music
  In the gushing of a rill;
There's music
  In all things, if men had ears:
Their earth
  Is but an echo of the spheres."

—George Gordon, Lord Byron

NEWPORT BAY
Door County, Wisconsin
Darryl R. Beers Photography

Country
CHRONICLE
Lansing Christman

WATER MUSIC

When I lived in upstate New York, I anticipated my yearly Thanksgiving ritual—a walk along a half-mile creek that wound through our woods, across a meadow, and finally beside a pasture before reaching the backyard of our home. Living now in South Carolina, I follow the path only in my memories; and with each Thanksgiving, I give thanks to God for that experience.

My yearly walk guided me along the familiar stream that I knew as the "crick" when I was a boy. Although I am careful to call them creeks now, it really doesn't matter. They all sing, and their songs are therapy for the spirit and the soul.

It was a joy to walk along the bank of our creek each year and listen to the music of the bubbling waters. I would see the pollywogs and frogs, the tadpoles and crayfish. On exceptionally warm Thanksgiving days, I could stick my feet in the water to let the minnows tickle my toes.

Not far from the house, the creek fell into two small waterfalls. How I loved the music of water pouring over the falls and curling around the stones. Here were the oldest musical instruments in the world, the oldest orchestras playing the oldest symphonies. God raised His baton, and the music began.

How often in the waters I have heard the music of the composers. At times, I would think of Vivaldi's "Four Seasons." On other days, I would dream of Debussy's "Claire de Lune" or "Afternoon of a Fawn," soothing as a day in glorious autumn. I could imagine I was hearing Tchaikovsky's Piano Concerto, like the drenching rains that nourish the earth.

I am now too far away and no longer hear the creek's glorious music on Thanksgiving Day. Although the songs have ended, the melody still lingers on in my memory; and I will forever be thankful.

The author of two published books, Lansing Christman has been contributing to Ideals *for more than twenty years. Mr. Christman has also been published in several American, foreign, and braille anthologies. He lives in rural South Carolina.*

TOMS BRANCH FALLS
Great Smoky Mountains National Park, Tennessee
Adam Jones Photography

Attic Treasure

Lucile B. Davis

I found an attic trunk today,
    All covered, thick with dust.
At last I got it open,
    Though its clasp was brown with rust.

Music, sheets and sheets of it,
    I found to my delight;
And though each page was yellowed now,
    The notes were clear and bright.

I saw the hymns my mother sang;
    A lump came to my throat.
I almost heard her sweet, clear voice
    In each beloved note.

The war songs were the next ones found;
    They brought remembered pride
And heartaches as I'd said good-bye,
    An anxious, tearful bride.

"K-K-K-Katy," "Over There,"
    And "Tipperary" too.
We'd packed up all our troubles
    In the kit bag, tried and true.

And oh, such happy tunes were next;
    I dried my misty eyes.
My Johnny had come marching home,
    And then were lullabies.

My old-time favorites filled the trunk—
    "A Bicycle Built for Two,"
Then "Always" and "Remember"
    And old "Rhapsody in Blue."

Recital pieces, Christmas songs;
    The hours sped away,
And each one brought a mem'ry
    Of a long-forgotten day.

"White Christmas" brought back memories
    Of one more hard-won fight.
Our sons had served with honor
    For their country, home, and right.

Sweet songs of home and apple trees
    And bluebirds over Dover,
And lights to come back on again,
    A peaceful world all over.

My dear great-grandson found me there;
    He seemed to understand.
He gathered up the music
    And then took me by the hand.

He led me gently down the stairs
    And stayed awhile to play;
The old piano rang with all
    The songs of yesterday.

I smiled and listened as he played
    A song so bright and new,
A modern one so different;
    And yet I loved it too.

I watched his fingers stroke the keys;
    I saw his dark head bowed.
I knew he wove his memories
    And almost said aloud,

"Perhaps in years to come you'll hear
    Some long forgotten strain,
And mem'ries of these hours we've shared
    Today will still remain.

And as the songs you cherish now
    Combine with mine, you'll see
They'll blend themselves together
    Into perfect harmony."

MUSICAL MEMORIE
Herb Stormo
Unicorn Stock Phot

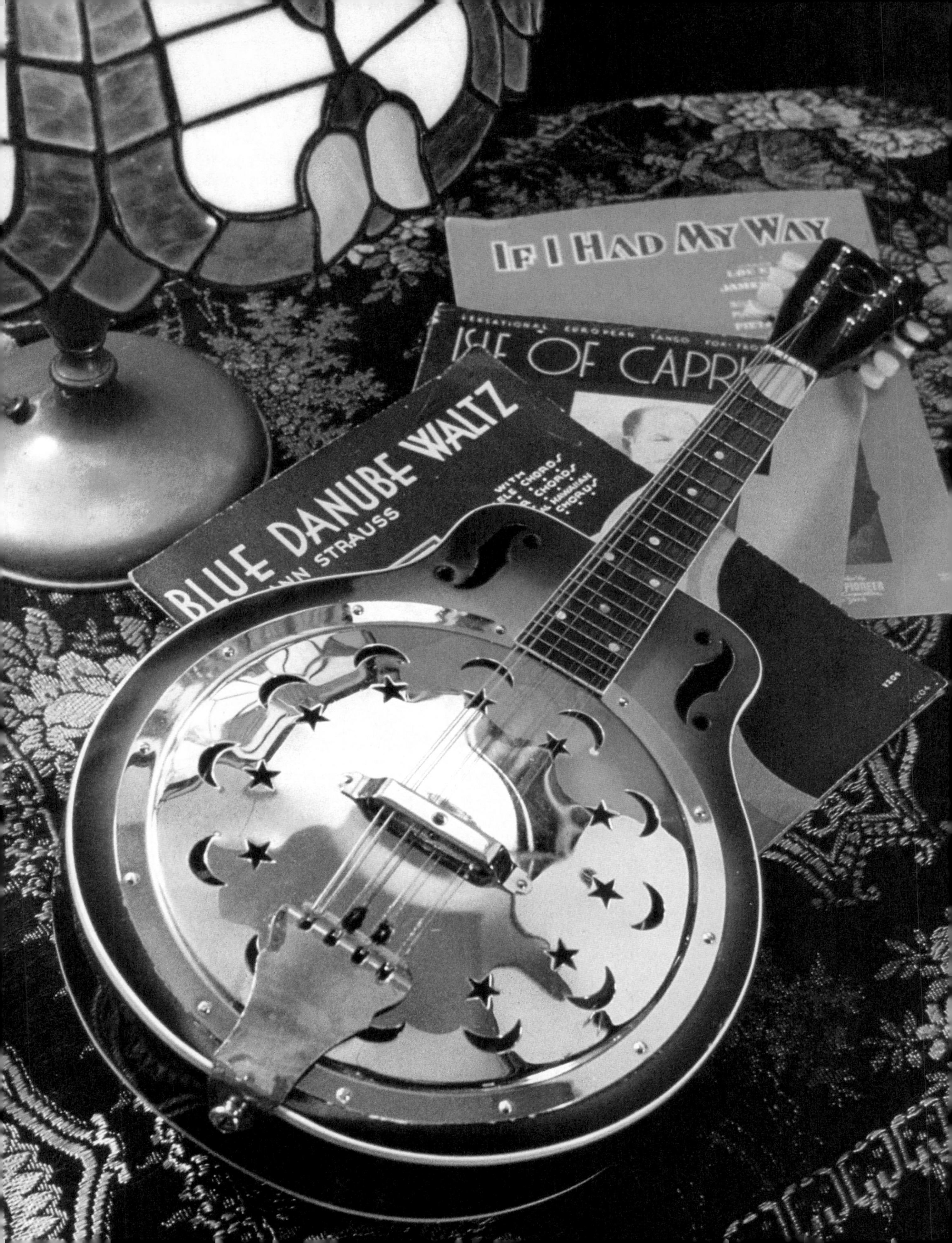
IF I HAD MY WAY
ISLE OF
BLUE DANUBE WALTZ
STRAUSS

SHEET MUSIC

by Connie Flood

On a recent holiday trip to my parents' home, I decided to sift through some of the clutter that always accumulates in the nooks and crannies of a home with a busy family like mine. I opened up the antique piano bench and was greeted by the familiar, musty smell of long-saved sheet music. As I dug through the piles of music and marveled at the seemingly endless capacity of our piano bench, I remembered those afternoons of my childhood when I would sit at the piano for hours, dutifully plunking out everything from "Twinkle, Twinkle, Little Star" to waltzes by Chopin. At the very bottom of the bench, underneath the stacks of classical music required for my piano lessons, I discovered a collection of the popular songs I loved as a child—songs that were reserved for the free time that remained after I had finished the music required for my lessons. Some of it was music I had bought myself with my allowance; and I laughed as I thumbed through the fancy, bright title pages of the sheet music, adorned with the pictures of the singers and bands I had heard on the radio when I was young. Mixed in with this youthful display was another group of sheet music with crumbling corners and fading covers, music that my great-aunt Jennie had given to me when I first began playing the piano. This was Aunt Jennie's own collection of popular music from her youth;

COLLECTIBLE SHEET MUSIC.
All images courtesy *The Sheet Music Reference & Price Guide, Second Edition,* by Anna Marie Guiheen & Marie-Reine A. Pafik, Collector Books.

and as a child, I prized it as much as the music I bought myself. I was just as likely to play a rousing rendition of "Over There" as a ballad by a pop singer.

My fascination with old sheet music carried over into my adulthood, and I now spend hours exploring antique stores and used book shops. I love to browse through boxes, crates, or filing cabinets full of forgotten sheet music and admire the beautiful title page illustrations and the photographs of famous singers and movie stars of days gone by. Every once in a while, I find a piece of music I simply must have; and I add it to my collection. My prized addition was a piece found in a box of sheet music I bought at a yard sale. At the very bottom was a first edition of the sheet music to "Somewhere Over the Rainbow," complete with an autographed picture of Judy Garland, who has always been one of my favorite actresses. I now keep it carefully stored with the rest of my old sheet music, but I always put it out on display for company.

When I left my parents' home at the end of my vacation, I had a few more additions to my collection—the sheet music my aunt Jennie had given me so many years ago. Although the pages are tattered and faded and probably not worth much to other sheet music collectors, I cherish this music's place in my childhood memories; and Aunt Jennie's favorite selections now have a new place of honor—right next to my prized Judy Garland sheet music whenever company comes to call.

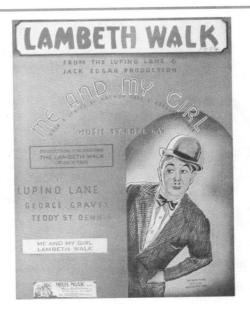

NOTEWORTHY

If you would like to start a collection of sheet music, here are some "noteworthy" facts you will want to know:

HISTORY

- Sheet music has been around for centuries, but the first American sheet music appeared around the time of the American Revolution.
- The first form of American sheet music was called a *broadside* and consisted of written lyrics sung to a popular tune and sold predominantly on street corners.
- Before 1920, sheet music was printed on large, 13½-by-10½-inch sheets called *folios*. Following 1920, it was printed on 9-by-12-inch paper.
- Sheet music was extremely popular in America until the advent of television in the 1950s. Music was sold in all types of stores, including drugstores and newsstands.
- Though many pieces are inexpensive to collect, demand for certain pieces is high. In 1988, a piece called "Home Run Polka" was sold at auction for $1,200.

FOCUSING COLLECTIONS

Because there is such a huge volume of sheet music from which to choose, collectors might wish to limit their collections to a particular theme. Some examples include:

- The work of a particular cover artist, such as Norman Rockwell
- The work of a particular composer, such as George Gershwin or Irving Berlin
- Pieces with photographs of a particular singer or actor, such as Shirley Temple or Bing Crosby
- Pieces about a particular subject or event, such as songs about World War II
- Pieces from a particular era, such as the 1920s or the 1940s
- Songs from a particular genre, such as jazz pieces or marches
- Autographed pieces signed by actors, singers, or composers

CARE

- Pieces with cellophane tape on them should be avoided, since the tape can discolor both the music to which it is attached and any music stored next to it.
- For best preservation, sheet music should be placed in unsealed plastic bags and stored in a dark place.
- Sheet music can be displayed, but long-term exposure to sunlight or fluorescent light can cause it to fade and crumble.

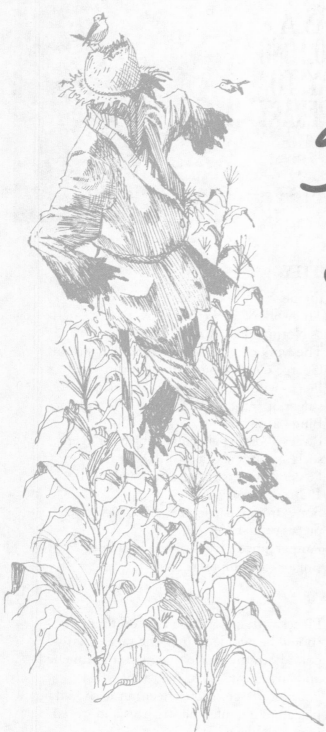

Winter Feast

Joy E. Merkley

I watched the migrant robin
On the pyracantha bough
Indulge himself in such a feast.
I contemplated how
The principles of flight
Could ever operate for him;
For nineteen berries, in the hold,
Had filled him to the brim.
And when he flew away, ere long,
I laughed to see him go;
Though fully fueled for his next flight,
The take-off speed was slow.

FALL BRILLIANCE—CARDINAL
Susan Bourdet, artist
Courtesy of the artist and Wild Wings, Inc
Lake City, Minnesota

From My Garden Journal

by Deana Deck

PYRACANTHA

I have always found it interesting that so many vibrant reds, oranges, and yellows of fall-blooming plants perfectly complement the glow of brilliant color in the autumn landscape. Pumpkins, persimmons, buckthorn, chrysanthemums, orange-eye butterfly bush, cotoneaster, yellow sage, oleander, crepe myrtle, pyracantha, and many others all produce either berries, fruit, or blooms in what we think of as "traditional" fall colors.

One of the most vibrantly colored and versatile of these contributors to late season color is the pyracantha. Like many other colorful fall shrubs, pyracantha provides two-season interest. It actually blooms in spring, producing blossoms of white or creamy ivory, depending on the species. These spring blooms are not the pyracantha's most memorable performance, however. In the fall, the plant produces an abundance of berries in bright, bird-attracting colors that range from yellow through all the oranges and on into a variety of red shades. A collection of berry-laden pyracantha branches offers the perfect display of autumn color and can make a stunning centerpiece for the Thanksgiving table.

You can find a wide variety of pyracanthas in most temperate parts of the country, but the majority are cold-tolerant only to areas where winter temperatures never drop below -10° F. Species in this classification include the popular but disease-prone Scarlet Firethorn (*Pyracantha coccina*) and its more disease-resistant cousin, the Lalandei. If you live in a cool climate, planting one of these varieties along a sunny south or east wall will provide protection against prevailing winds in winter.

For those who live in more northern areas, three hardier varieties are recommended: Lalandie and Thornless (*P. coccina*) both have red berries; and Kasan (*P. coccina*) bears deep-orange berries. Southern gardeners have more options, one of the most popular being the orange-red Japanese species known as the Formose Firethorn (*P. koidzumi*).

Pyracantha tolerates a wide range of soil types, with the exception of sandy or boggy conditions. In fact, studies indicate that pyracantha grown in sandy soil is more prone to fire blight, the great disease scourge of the species. Happily, this plant is easily hybridized, and many varieties have been introduced that are blight resistant. Among the best disease-resistant *P. coccina* cultivars are the American hybrids Mojave, Navaho, and Teton for orange berries, and Shawnee for yellow berries. Seek them out to save yourself a lot of time with the sprayer, especially if you live in a sandy, coastal area.

Another of pyracantha's virtues is that it is a

fast-growing evergreen (or semi-evergreen, depending on the climate) that will quickly fill in blank spaces in the landscape. Of course, some gardeners consider this a drawback, since the shrub requires annual heavy pruning and constant shaping to keep it in bounds. If left on its own, it will quickly form an impenetrable, thorny barrier that makes a beautiful fence. Just be sure to purchase a good pair of heavy-duty, leather garden gloves with your pyracantha; you'll need them for protection while transplanting as well as when pruning!

Don't let the pyracantha's thorns and growth rate deter you, however. The other side of the story is that pyracantha takes well to hard pruning, is easily trained into myriad shapes, and is one of the most popular plants in the landscape for espalier—the art of training a plant against a flat trellis to shape growth into a single plane. Espaliering is fun, creates an attractive focal point against an otherwise blank wall or fence, and requires only periodic effort.

In selecting a pyracantha for espalier, go against the normal inclination to purchase the largest shrub available in your budget range. Young, small, flexible plants are the best to start with. The most popular style of espalier is a traditional horizontal T shape where four to five branches on each side of a single trunk are trained along horizontal wires, similar to grape cultivation. If you plan to have more than one plant in the pattern, space them at least eight feet apart. To start, stretch four wires between two upright supports or build a frame against a wall. Be sure to allow a space of at least six inches between the supports and the wall to encourage healthy air circulation.

Plant a single whip, and support it with a vertical stake until it has grown to reach the lowest wire on the support or the bottom of the trellis. Cut the whip at this height, being sure to leave at least three strong-looking buds. The cuts should be about a quarter of an inch above the top bud. Subsequent growth will be concen-

Espaliering is fun, creates an attractive focal point against an otherwise blank wall or fence, and requires only periodic effort.

trated in the remaining buds. Select two to train horizontally to the left and right along the wires or trellis and guide one shoot straight up to become the leader. Remove all remaining shoots that appear. The following spring, before sap begins to flow, repeat the process at the second wire.

Meanwhile, train the horizontal branches by using the same three-bud technique: select one to become the horizontal leader, and two as side shoots. Remove any shoots that do not contribute to the pattern. Using this technique, it will take four years to complete the pattern, but you will be able to enjoy it for many years. More details on creating this and other patterns can be found in most pruning manuals or in books such as *Living Fences* by Ogden Tanner.

Pyracantha is such a rewarding plant to grow. Not only does it offer some of the richest and most stunning colors in autumn's palette, but with a little training from a patient gardener and some knowledge of espaliers, it becomes its own work of art. Once you select a bouquet of its colorful boughs for your Thanksgiving table, you'll surely agree that pyracantha is the perfect complement to nature's glorious fall production.

Deana Deck tends to her flowers, plants, and vegetables at her home in Nashville, Tennessee, where her popular garden column is a regular feature in The Tennessean.

Remember When

GRANDMOTHER'S ROSE JAR
Agnes M. Pharo

When I was a child, a jar of imprisoned summer graced the mantelpiece in my grandmother's home. Decorated with dainty, handpainted flowers, the fragile rose jar was filled with Grandmother's own blend of potpourri and opened for an hour at a time to freshen the room.

Sometimes I was allowed to lift the lid by its delicate china handle shaped like a beautiful rose—what sheer magic, especially on a chilly November day! The aroma that drifted out came straight from the Arabian Nights. It conjured up visions of rain-sweet gardens and spice-laden ships from the Orient. It was a magic carpet transporting me back to summer when bees droned in red hollyhocks and a thousand perfumes filled the air.

To my delight, Grandmother often let me help her

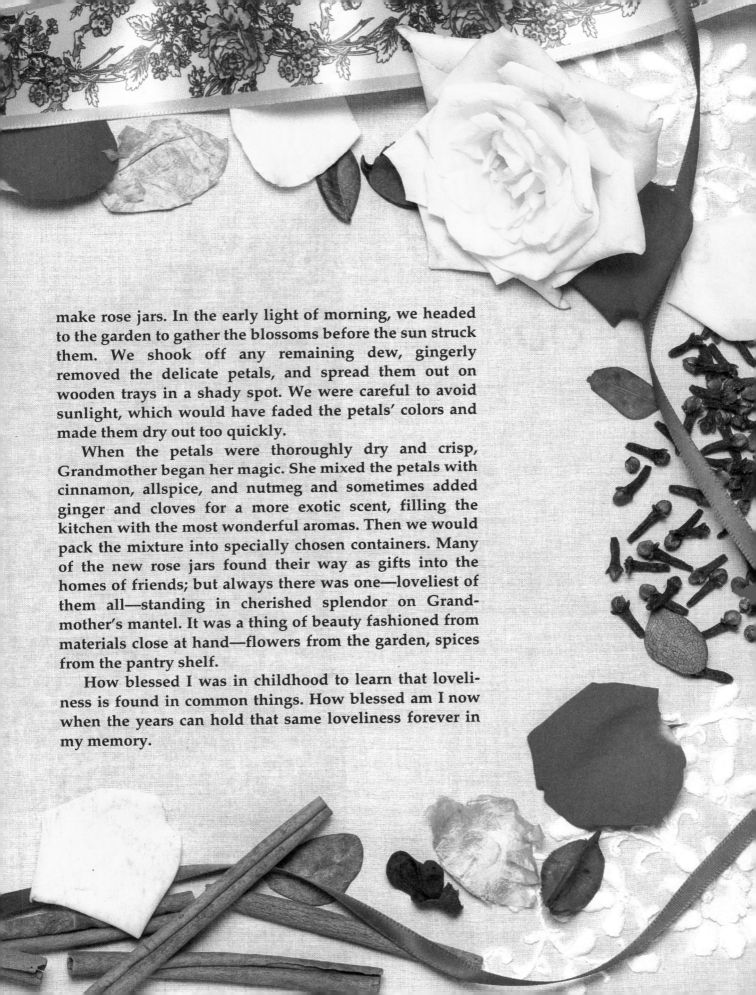

make rose jars. In the early light of morning, we headed to the garden to gather the blossoms before the sun struck them. We shook off any remaining dew, gingerly removed the delicate petals, and spread them out on wooden trays in a shady spot. We were careful to avoid sunlight, which would have faded the petals' colors and made them dry out too quickly.

When the petals were thoroughly dry and crisp, Grandmother began her magic. She mixed the petals with cinnamon, allspice, and nutmeg and sometimes added ginger and cloves for a more exotic scent, filling the kitchen with the most wonderful aromas. Then we would pack the mixture into specially chosen containers. Many of the new rose jars found their way as gifts into the homes of friends; but always there was one—loveliest of them all—standing in cherished splendor on Grandmother's mantel. It was a thing of beauty fashioned from materials close at hand—flowers from the garden, spices from the pantry shelf.

How blessed I was in childhood to learn that loveliness is found in common things. How blessed am I now when the years can hold that same loveliness forever in my memory.

The Woodland Pool

Rose Koralewsky

I love this pool where yellow lilies float,
    Mirrored in ebon glass;
Far in whose depths, unsullied and remote,
    I see the white clouds pass.

The scarlet torches of the maples burn
    Along its winding shores;
Above, ascending slowly, turn on turn,
    A hawk in silence soars.

The brooding Spirit of the wilderness
    Murmurs of rest and peace;
All petty griefs and nagging cares that press
    Their fretful torment cease.

After the bright blue fervor of the day,
    The night is sweet and cool;
Softly, with thoughts that venerate and pray,
    I leave the woodland pool.

AUTUMN REFLECTIONS
Sugar Hill, New Hampshire
Dianne Dietrich Leis Photography

Something Told the Wild Geese

Rachel Field

Something told the wild geese
    It was time to go.
Though the fields lay golden,
    Something whispered, "Snow."

Leaves were green and stirring,
    Berries, luster-glossed,
But beneath warm feathers
    Something cautioned, "Frost."

All the sagging orchards
    Steamed with amber spice,
But each wild breast stiffened
    At remembered ice.

Something told the wild geese
    It was time to fly,
Summer sun was on their wings,
    Winter in their cry.

GOLDEN BOUNTY—CANADA GEESE
David A. Maass, artist
Courtesy of the artist and Wild Wings, Inc.
Lake City, Minnesota

A Prayer

Adelaide Love

Not only in my summer let me sing
When beauty storms my senses and my soul,
When mine is the mysterious and dark
Delight of one who feels the quivering,
Tumultuous heart surrender utterly,
Idolatrous of that bright deity.
Let me not ever lose the moment when
I stand, transfigured, on the shining verge
Of dreams beyond all telling and I glimpse
The realm where earth and heaven subtly merge.
O God, when in my winter I shall walk
The quiet and the twilight ways along,
Let me feel still a breath upon my brow
And find in snow the silver seeds of song.

SNOW-DUSTED FOLIAGE
Adam Jones Photography

Readers' Forum

Meet Our Ideals Readers and Their Families

We are happy to share this photograph sent to us by MARYLAVON LEMLER of Fort Wayne, Indiana. Last fall, Marylavon's neighbor, James Shepherrd, looked out his kitchen window one night and was surprised to see that a large, bright-eyed, furry opossum had taken up residency in Marylavon's bird feeder. She says that where the opossum came from and how it was able to get in and out of the tall feeder have always been a delightful mystery.

SARA DAVIS of Springfield, Ohio, shares with us this picture of her happy granddaughter Hannah Elisabeth Davis enjoying autumn's splendor when she was six months old. Sara tells us that Hannah is still enchanted by the outdoors and loves to be outside when she visits her grandparents from her home in Circleville, Ohio. Among Hannah's favorite activities are donning hats and riding on the tractor with "papaw."

MINNIE KATHERINE LANE of Franklin, Wisconsin, has sent us this wonderful photo of her great-grand-daughter Olivia Katherine Brewer decked out in full trick-or-treat regalia. Olivia, age one and a half years, lives in Oak Creek, Wisconsin, and is one of fourteen grandchildren and great-grandchildren of whom Minnie and her husband Herb are extremely proud! Minnie tells us that although the family is quite large, they are very close and always gather together for holidays and special events.

THANK YOU Marylavon Lemler, Sara Davis, and Minnie Katherine Lane for sharing with *Ideals*. We hope to hear from other readers who would like to share photos and stories with the Ideals family. Please include a self-addressed, stamped envelope if you would like the photos returned. Keep your original photographs for safekeeping and send duplicate photos along with your name, address, and telephone number to:

READERS' FORUM
IDEALS PUBLICATIONS INC.
P.O. BOX 305300
NASHVILLE, TENNESSEE 37230

Publisher, Patricia A. Pingry
Editor, Lisa C. Ragan
Copy Editor, Michelle Prater Burke
Electronic Prepress, Anne Lesemann
Editorial Assistant, Brian L. Bacon
Editorial Intern, Connie Flood
Contributing Editors,
Lansing Christman, Deana Deck, Russ Flint,
Pamela Kennedy, Patrick McRae, Mary
Skarmeas, Nancy Skarmeas

ACKNOWLEDGMENTS

SOMETHING TOLD THE WILD GEESE by Rachel Field. Used by permission of the author's estate. MY NOVEMBER GUEST from *THE COLLECTED POEMS OF ROBERT FROST* by Robert Frost, copyright © 1930 by Henry Holt and Company, Inc., copyright © 1936 by Robert Frost. Reprinted by permission of Henry Holt and Co., Inc. RAISIN PIE from *A HEAP O' LIVIN'* by Edgar A. Guest, copyright © 1926 by The Reilly & Lee Co. Used by permission of the author's estate. THE WOODLAND POOL from *NEW ENGLAND HERITAGE AND OTHER POEMS* by Rose Koralewsky. Used by permission of Branden Publishing, Boston. PRAYER FOR LITTLE THINGS from *THE SHINING THREAD* by Jessie Wilmore Murton. Reprinted by permission of Pacific Press Publishing Association. LATE AUTUMN from *AGAINST ALL TIME* by Isla Paschal Richardson. Used by permission of Branden Publishing, Boston. THEME IN YELLOW from *EARLY MOON* by Carl Sandburg, copyright © 1930 by Harcourt Brace & Company and renewed 1958 by Carl Sandburg, reprinted by permission of the publisher. NOVEMBER from *STILLMEADOW CALENDAR* by Gladys Taber, copyright © 1967 by Gladys Taber. All rights reserved. Reprinted with permission of Brandt & Brandt Literary Agents, Inc. Our sincere thanks to the following authors whom we were unable to contact: Adelaide Love for A PRAYER, Anna M. Priestley for BORROWED BEAUTY, and Violet Alleyn Storey for IN A FIELD OF BITTERSWEET.

CHOOSE THE PERFECT GIFT FROM SOME OF THESE BEAUTIFUL *ideals* BOOKS

NEW

AMERICAN FAMILY TREASURY
(160 pages, hardcover)
$19.95
Order 40490A

AMERICA CELEBRATES
(160 pages, hardcover)
$19.95
Order 40717A

IDEALS 50TH ANNIVERSARY COLLECTOR'S EDITION
(80 pages, hardcover)
$9.95
Order 11261A

GOD'S BEAUTIFUL WORLD
(160 pages, hardcover)
$19.95
Order 40520A

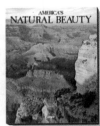

AMERICA'S NATURAL BEAU
(160 pages, hardcover)
$19.95
Order 40482A

THE GIFT OF FRIENDSHIP
(160 pages, hardcover)
$19.95
Order 40709A

IDEALS FRIENDSHIP
(88 pages, softcover)
$5.95
Order 11393A

5-PACK OF IDEALS FRIENDSHIP — great for hostess gifts, birthdays, or a special remembrance. Comes with gift envelopes.
$20.95
Order 52170A

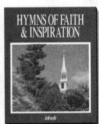

PRAYERS AND POEMS OF INSPIRATION
(160 pages, hardcover)
$19.95
Order 40474A

HYMNS OF FAITH & INSPIRATION
(160 pages, hardcover)
$19.95
Order 40415A

FOOTSTE

IN THE FOOTST THE MAST
(160 pages, ha
$19.95
Order 404.

NEW

COLLECTOR'S EDITION
JOLLY OLD SANTA CLAUS

Now, 35 years after its first publication, here is the original story of Jolly Old Santa, Mrs. Claus, and all the elves. Through modern technology, the exquisite oil paintings of George Hinke are as vibrant as the originals. Take your favorite youngster on a tour of the North Pole with a book that is loved by children everywhere.

(32 colorful pages, hardbound cover, dustjacket)
$14.95
Order 40806A

PRAYERS & POEMS FOR CHRISTMAS
(160 pages, hardcover)
$19.95
Order 40741A

VICTORY
(80 pages, hardcover)
$9.95
Order 40687A

THE HERITAC

THE HERIT OF AMER
(160 pages, ha
$19.95
Order 405

CHRISTMAS MEMORIES
(48 pages, hardcover)
$14.95
Order 77025A

THE CAROLS OF CHRISTMAS
(160 pages, hardcover)
$19.95
Order 40547A

5-PACK OF IDEALS CHRISTMAS — Share the delight of Christmastime with your friends and family when you order a 5-pack. Comes with gift envelopes.
$20.95
Order 52200A

IDEALS CHRISTMAS
(88 pages, softcover)
$5.95
Order 11415A

SLIPCASE HOLDS 1 FULL YEAR OF IDEALS
$9.95
Order 10796

If order totals $25 or more, you receive **A FREE GIFT!**

Please make sure order envelope is sealed; use tape o staples if necessar

FOR FURTHER INFORMATION OR TO ORDER BY CREDIT CARD, PLEASE CALL TOLL-FREE 1-800-558-4
For Christmas delivery, we must receive your order by December 5
We're sorry, but we are unable to ship orders outside the United States.

RUSH!
CHRISTMAS
ORDER

PLACE
STAMP
HERE

IDEALS PUBLICATIONS INCORPORATED
P.O. Box 305300
Nashville, TN 37230-5300

DON'T FORGET THE YOUNGSTERS
ON YOUR LIST!

Give them our *brand new* collector's edition of
the beloved Ideals children's classic, *Jolly Old
Santa Claus,* with the masterful oil paintings of
George Hinke. Supply is limited!

Retail price . . . $16.95
Your price $14.95

CHRISTMAS ORDER FORM

ORDER #	ITEM	# TO ME	TO GIFT A	TO GIFT B	UNIT PRICE	TOTAL PRICE
40490A	American Family Treasury				$19.95	
40717A	America Celebrates **NEW**				$19.95	
11261A	50th Anniversary				$ 9.95	
07806A	50th Anniversary—5-pack				$39.95	
40520A	God's Beautiful World				$19.95	
40482A	America's Natural Beauty				$19.95	
40709A	Gift of Friendship				$19.95	
11393A	Ideals Friendship				$ 5.95	
52170A	Ideals Friendship—5-pack				$20.95	
40474A	Prayers & Poems/ Inspiration				$19.95	
40415A	Hymns of Faith & Inspiration				$19.95	
40431A	In the Footsteps/ Master				$19.95	
40806A	Jolly Old Santa Claus **NEW**				$14.95	
40741A	Prayers & Poems/Christmas				$19.95	
40687A	Victory				$ 9.95	
52057A	Victory—5-pack				$39.95	
40598A	Heritage of America				$19.95	
85672A	Christmas Memories				$14.95	
40547A	Carols of Christmas				$19.95	
11415A	Ideals Christmas				$ 5.95	
52200A	Ideals Christmas—5-pack				$20.95	
10796	Ideals Slipcase				$ 9.95	

BOOK TOTAL	$
Tennessee Residents Add 8.25% State Tax.	$
SUBTOTAL	$
SHIPPING & HANDLING	$
TOTAL AMOUNT	$

Shipping for each address is $3.50 in the USA plus $.50 for each item over 4 items.

If order totals $25 or more, you receive A FREE GIFT!

ORDER MUST INCLUDE PAYMENT IN U.S. DOLLARS
Minimum order is $10.00. All orders subject to approval.
Sorry, we cannot ship orders outside the U.S.

To ensure Christmas delivery,
we must receive your order not later than December 5.

**FOR INFORMATION
OR FASTER SERVICE
CALL TOLL FREE
1-800-558-4343**

HOW TO ORDER

Fill in name, address, and method of payment below. If paying by credit card, include account number, expiration date, and signature. On the order blank opposite, indicate the quantity of items ordered in the appropriate column. The number to be sent to your address, the number to Gift Name A and to Gift Name B. Total your order; add shipping, handling, and sales tax, if applicable. Include your check or money order in the envelope. Seal, stamp, and mail.

Name

Address

City   State   ZIP

Gift Name **A**

Address

City   State   ZIP

Gift Name **B**

Address

City   State   ZIP

Check enclosed ☐   MasterCard ☐   VISA ☐   DISCOVER ☐

Account #

Expiration Date

Tel. Area Code   Telephone #

Signature